Story Starte

Grades 4-6

Written by Veneda Murtha
Illustrated by S&S Learning Materials

ISBN 978-1-55035-779-4
Copyright 2005
Revised February 2007
All Rights Reserved * Printed in Canada

Permission to Reproduce

Published in the United States by:
On The Mark Press
3909 Witmer Road PMB 175
Niagara Falls, New York
14305
www.onthemarkpress.com

Published in Canada by:
S&S Learning Materials
15 Dairy Avenue
Napanee, Ontario
K7R 1M4
www.sslearning.com

At  Glance

Learning Expectations

Through the meaningful context of creative writing, students will:

✔ Interpret a variety of illustrations, using evidence from the images and their own knowledge and experience

✔ Develop ability in creative, independent thinking, and ordering of ideas in a logical manner

✔ Communicate their ideas clearly and effectively

✔ Communicate their ideas for specific purposes and to specific audiences

✔ Apply previously learned basic skills of grammar, spelling, punctuation, and conventions of style and form

✔ Practice proofreading and editing skills

Story Starters

Table of Contents

Story Starters

Introduction

Why Use this Resource

Congratulations on your purchase of a worthwhile classroom resource! This collection of 58 engaging and detailed illustrations will inspire students' creative writing. Images of varying complexities are included so that students with a wide range of critical thinking and writing abilities may engage meaningfully with them. The illustrations may be used as "starters" for a variety of forms of writing, and can be used to augment any writing program. Or, use them as a meaningful "filler" activity when students have extra classroom time.

Organization of the Book

This resource is divided into four sections based on the primary story genre of the illustrations:

1.	General Fiction	3.	Historical
2.	Adventure	4.	Fantasy

For easy reference, the story genre and illustration number are listed at the bottom of each page.

Each story starter worksheet includes an illustration and blank word box, a blank line for the story's title, and numbered blank lines for the story itself. The word box provides space for students to brainstorm key words that come to mind when they explore their overall impression of the illustration. Students should complete the brainstorm list before writing to stimulate their creative thinking. The blank lines are numbered so that you may easily give students instructions on how long their creative writing piece should be.

A blank lined page is included at the back of this book (page 64) and may be used to write a story outline, or to continue writing the story itself if the student needs extra space.

Students may be given the Editing Checklist and Proofreader's Marks (page 5) either before or after writing a story. The checklist is a useful guide for proofreading their stories, and the chart of proofreader's marks lists the commonly used symbols, or shorthand, and their meanings.

How to Use the Illustrations

The story starters may be used as springboards for a variety of forms of creative writing. The most straightforward use is for a short story. Students who would benefit from other writing challenges may enjoy using the story starters to write any of the following:

- Poetry
- Biography or autobiography of a character in the illustration
- A letter written to or from a character
- Newspaper article or editorial about the event or issue represented in the illustration
- Diary or personal journal entry of a character
- Script for a play or movie
- And many other forms of writing!

Name: _____

Story Title: _____

Editing Checklist

Put a check mark next to the item once you have checked your writing and are satisfied that it is true.

◯ All verbs are in the same tense, either past or present.

◯ Each sentence begins with a capital letter and ends with the proper punctuation (period, question mark or exclamation mark).

◯ Direct speech of characters begins and ends with quotations marks. (**Example**: "Hello," she said.)

◯ Apostrophes are used in the correct position in words to indicate possession. (**Examples**: the boy's bike, the boys' bikes)

◯ All words are spelled correctly.

◯ All sentences are complete.

◯ There are no run-on sentences.

◯ The first sentence of each new paragraph is indented.

Proofreader's Marks

Mark	Meaning
⊙	Add a period
︿	Add a comma
∧	Add a word or letter
∨	Add an apostrophe
ᵛᵛ	Add quotation marks
ℓ	Remove
͜	Take out the space

Mark	Meaning
#	Put in a space
≡	Change to a capital letter
/	Change to a lower case letter
¶	Begin a new paragraph
⌐	Indent the line (to begin a new paragraph)
SP	Spelling error

Name: _____

(Title) _____

Brainstorm Word List

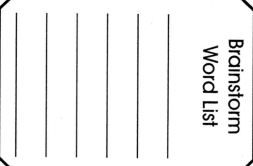

1 _____

2 _____

3 _____

4 _____

5 _____

6 _____

7 _____

8 _____

9 _____

10 _____

11 _____

12 _____

13 _____

14 _____

15 _____

General Fiction - Illustration 1

OTM-1865 • SSR1-65 Story Starters

Name: _____

Brainstorm
Word List

_____
(Title)

1 _____

2 _____

3 _____

4 _____

5 _____

6 _____

7 _____

8 _____

9 _____

10 _____

11 _____

12 _____

13 _____

14 _____

15 _____

Name: _____

_____
(Title)

Brainstorm Word List

1 _____

2 _____

3 _____

4 _____

5 _____

6 _____

7 _____

8 _____

9 _____

10 _____

11 _____

12 _____

13 _____

14 _____

15 _____

Story Starters

Name: _____

Brainstorm
Word List

_____

_____

_____

_____

_____

_____

_____ (Title)

1 _____

2 _____

3 _____

4 _____

5 _____

6 _____

7 _____

8 _____

9 _____

10 _____

11 _____

12 _____

13 _____

14 _____

15 _____

Name: _____

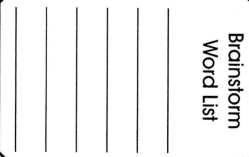

Brainstorm Word List

_____ (Title)

1 _____
2 _____
3 _____
4 _____
5 _____
6 _____
7 _____
8 _____
9 _____
10 _____
11 _____
12 _____
13 _____
14 _____
15 _____

Story Starters

Name: _____

Brainstorm
Word List

_____
_____
_____
_____
_____
_____

_____
(Title)

1 _____
2 _____
3 _____
4 _____
5 _____
6 _____
7 _____
8 _____
9 _____
10 _____
11 _____
12 _____
13 _____
14 _____
15 _____

OTM-1865 • SSR1-65 Story Starters

11

Name: _____

Brainstorm
Word List

_____
(Title)

1 _____
2 _____
3 _____
4 _____
5 _____
6 _____
7 _____
8 _____
9 _____
10 _____
11 _____
12 _____
13 _____
14 _____
15 _____

General Fiction - Illustration 7

Name: _____

Brainstorm Word List

_____
(Title)

1 _____
2 _____
3 _____
4 _____
5 _____
6 _____
7 _____
8 _____
9 _____
10 _____
11 _____
12 _____
13 _____
14 _____
15 _____

General Fiction - Illustration 8

Name: _____

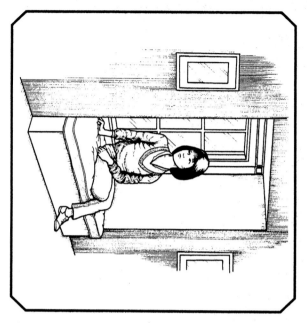

(Title) _____

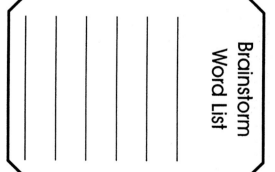

Brainstorm Word List

1 _____
2 _____
3 _____
4 _____
5 _____
6 _____
7 _____
8 _____
9 _____
10 _____
11 _____
12 _____
13 _____
14 _____
15 _____

Name: _____

Brainstorm
Word List

_____
(Title)

1 _____
2 _____
3 _____
4 _____
5 _____
6 _____
7 _____
8 _____
9 _____
10 _____
11 _____
12 _____
13 _____
14 _____
15 _____

General Fiction - Illustration 10

Name: _____

Brainstorm Word List

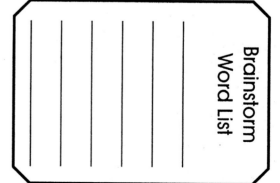

(Title) _____

1 _____

2 _____

3 _____

4 _____

5 _____

6 _____

7 _____

8 _____

9 _____

10 _____

11 _____

12 _____

13 _____

14 _____

15 _____

General Fiction - Illustration 11

Name: _____

Brainstorm
Word List

_____
(Title)

1 _____

2 _____

3 _____

4 _____

5 _____

6 _____

7 _____

8 _____

9 _____

10 _____

11 _____

12 _____

13 _____

14 _____

15 _____

Name: _____

_____
(Title)

Brainstorm Word List

1 _____

2 _____

3 _____

4 _____

5 _____

6 _____

7 _____

8 _____

9 _____

10 _____

11 _____

12 _____

13 _____

14 _____

15 _____

General Fiction - Illustration 13

Story Starters

Name: _____

Brainstorm
Word List

_____
_____
_____
_____
_____
_____

_____
(Title)

1 _____
2 _____
3 _____
4 _____
5 _____
6 _____
7 _____
8 _____
9 _____
10 _____
11 _____
12 _____
13 _____
14 _____
15 _____

General Fiction - Illustration 14

OTM-1865 • SSR1-65 Story Starters

Name: _____

Brainstorm
Word List

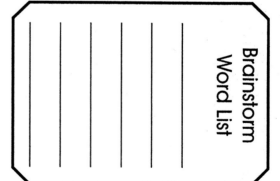

_____
(Title)

1 _____

2 _____

3 _____

4 _____

5 _____

6 _____

7 _____

8 _____

9 _____

10 _____

11 _____

12 _____

13 _____

14 _____

15 _____

General Fiction - Illustration 15

Name: _____

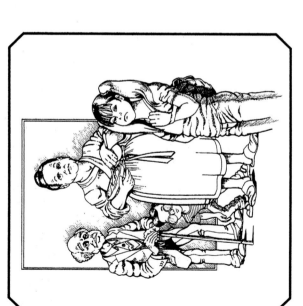

Brainstorm
Word List

_____
_____
_____
_____
_____
_____

_____ (Title)

1 _____

2 _____

3 _____

4 _____

5 _____

6 _____

7 _____

8 _____

9 _____

10 _____

11 _____

12 _____

13 _____

14 _____

15 _____

Name: _____

_____
(Title)

1 _____

2 _____

3 _____

4 _____

5 _____

6 _____

7 _____

8 _____

9 _____

10 _____

11 _____

12 _____

13 _____

14 _____

15 _____

Name: _____

Brainstorm
Word List

_____

_____

_____

_____

_____

_____

_____

(Title)

1 _____

2 _____

3 _____

4 _____

5 _____

6 _____

7 _____

8 _____

9 _____

10 _____

11 _____

12 _____

13 _____

14 _____

15 _____

Name: _____

_____
(Title)

Brainstorm Word List

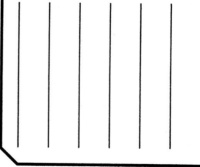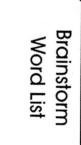

1 _____

2 _____

3 _____

4 _____

5 _____

6 _____

7 _____

8 _____

9 _____

10 _____

11 _____

12 _____

13 _____

14 _____

15 _____

Name: _____

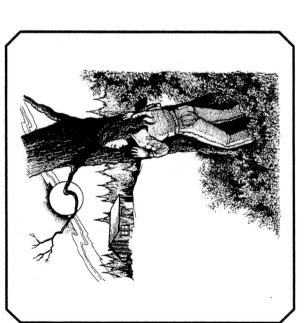

Brainstorm
Word List

_____
_____
_____
_____
_____

_____
(Title)

1 _____
2 _____
3 _____
4 _____
5 _____
6 _____
7 _____
8 _____
9 _____
10 _____
11 _____
12 _____
13 _____
14 _____
15 _____

Adventure - Illustration 20

Name: _____

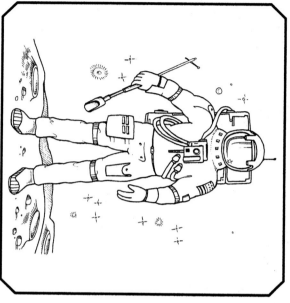

(Title) _____

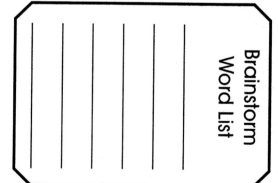

Brainstorm Word List

1 _____

2 _____

3 _____

4 _____

5 _____

6 _____

7 _____

8 _____

9 _____

10 _____

11 _____

12 _____

13 _____

14 _____

15 _____

Adventure - Illustration 21

Name: _____

Brainstorm
Word List

_____
(Title)

1 _____

2 _____

3 _____

4 _____

5 _____

6 _____

7 _____

8 _____

9 _____

10 _____

11 _____

12 _____

13 _____

14 _____

15 _____

Name: _____

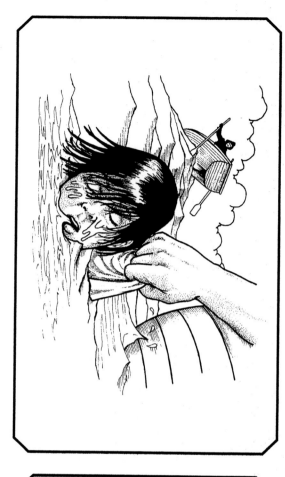

Brainstorm
Word List

_____
(Title)

1 _____

2 _____

3 _____

4 _____

5 _____

6 _____

7 _____

8 _____

9 _____

10 _____

11 _____

12 _____

13 _____

14 _____

15 _____

Adventure - Illustration 23

Story Starters

Name: _____

Brainstorm Word List

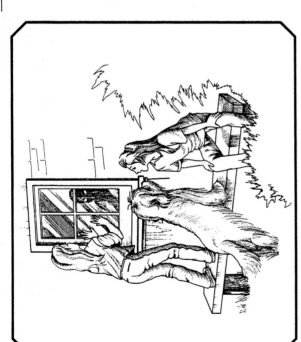

_____ (Title)

1. _____
2. _____
3. _____
4. _____
5. _____
6. _____
7. _____
8. _____
9. _____
10. _____
11. _____
12. _____
13. _____
14. _____
15. _____

Name: _____

(Title)

Brainstorm Word List

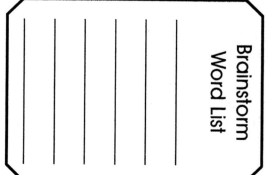

1 _____

2 _____

3 _____

4 _____

5 _____

6 _____

7 _____

8 _____

9 _____

10 _____

11 _____

12 _____

13 _____

14 _____

15 _____

Adventure - Illustration 25

Story Starters

Name: _____

Brainstorm Word List

_____
_____
_____
_____
_____
_____

(Title) _____

1 _____

2 _____

3 _____

4 _____

5 _____

6 _____

7 _____

8 _____

9 _____

10 _____

11 _____

12 _____

13 _____

14 _____

15 _____

Name: _____

(Title) _____

Brainstorm Word List

1. _____
2. _____
3. _____
4. _____
5. _____
6. _____
7. _____
8. _____
9. _____
10. _____
11. _____
12. _____
13. _____
14. _____
15. _____

Adventure - Illustration 27

Name: _____

Brainstorm Word List

_____
(Title)

1. _____
2. _____
3. _____
4. _____
5. _____
6. _____
7. _____
8. _____
9. _____
10. _____
11. _____
12. _____
13. _____
14. _____
15. _____

Name: _____

Brainstorm
Word List

_____ (Title)

1 _____

2 _____

3 _____

4 _____

5 _____

6 _____

7 _____

8 _____

9 _____

10 _____

11 _____

12 _____

13 _____

14 _____

15 _____

Adventure - Illustration 29

Story Starters

Name: _____

Brainstorm Word List

_____
_____
_____
_____
_____
_____

_____
(Title)

1 _____
2 _____
3 _____
4 _____
5 _____
6 _____
7 _____
8 _____
9 _____
10 _____
11 _____
12 _____
13 _____
14 _____
15 _____

Name: _____

_____
(Title)

Brainstorm Word List

1 _____
2 _____
3 _____
4 _____
5 _____
6 _____
7 _____
8 _____
9 _____
10 _____
11 _____
12 _____
13 _____
14 _____
15 _____

Adventure - Illustration 31

Story Starters

Name: _____

_____
(Title)

1 _____

2 _____

3 _____

4 _____

5 _____

6 _____

7 _____

8 _____

9 _____

10 _____

11 _____

12 _____

13 _____

14 _____

15 _____

OFM-1865 • SSR1-65 Story Starters

Adventure - Illustration 32

Name: _____

(Title) _____

1 _____

2 _____

3 _____

4 _____

5 _____

6 _____

7 _____

8 _____

9 _____

10 _____

11 _____

12 _____

13 _____

14 _____

15 _____

Brainstorm Word List

Historical - Illustration 33

Story Starters

Name: _____

Brainstorm
Word List

_____
_____
_____
_____
_____
_____

_____
(Title)

1 _____
2 _____
3 _____
4 _____
5 _____
6 _____
7 _____
8 _____
9 _____
10 _____
11 _____
12 _____
13 _____
14 _____
15 _____

Historical - Illustration 34

Name: _____

(Title) _____

Brainstorm Word List

1. _____
2. _____
3. _____
4. _____
5. _____
6. _____
7. _____
8. _____
9. _____
10. _____
11. _____
12. _____
13. _____
14. _____
15. _____

Historical - Illustration 35

Story Starters

Name: _____

Brainstorm
Word List

_____
_____
_____
_____
_____
_____

_____
(Title)

1 _____
2 _____
3 _____
4 _____
5 _____
6 _____
7 _____
8 _____
9 _____
10 _____
11 _____
12 _____
13 _____
14 _____
15 _____

41

Historical - Illustration 36

Name: _____

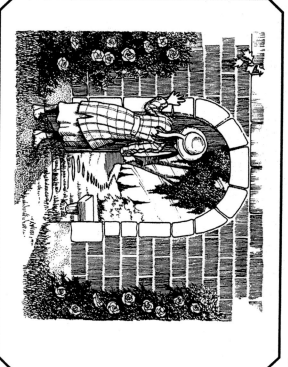

Brainstorm
Word List

_____ (Title)

1 _____

2 _____

3 _____

4 _____

5 _____

6 _____

7 _____

8 _____

9 _____

10 _____

11 _____

12 _____

13 _____

14 _____

15 _____

Story Starters

Name: _____

Brainstorm Word List

_____
_____
_____
_____
_____
_____

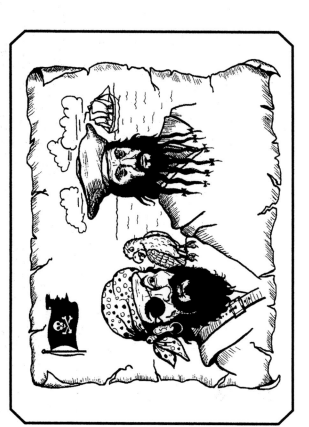

_____
(Title)

1 _____

2 _____

3 _____

4 _____

5 _____

6 _____

7 _____

8 _____

9 _____

10 _____

11 _____

12 _____

13 _____

14 _____

15 _____

43

Name: _____

Brainstorm
Word List

(Title) _____

1 _____

2 _____

3 _____

4 _____

5 _____

6 _____

7 _____

8 _____

9 _____

10 _____

11 _____

12 _____

13 _____

14 _____

15 _____

Story Starters

Name: _____

_____
(Title)

1 _____

2 _____

3 _____

4 _____

5 _____

6 _____

7 _____

8 _____

9 _____

10 _____

11 _____

12 _____

13 _____

14 _____

15 _____

Name: _____

_____
(Title)

Brainstorm
Word List

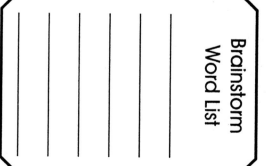

1 _____

2 _____

3 _____

4 _____

5 _____

6 _____

7 _____

8 _____

9 _____

10 _____

11 _____

12 _____

13 _____

14 _____

15 _____

Story Starters

Name: _____

Brainstorm
Word List

_____
_____
_____
_____
_____
_____

_____ (Title)

1 _____

2 _____

3 _____

4 _____

5 _____

6 _____

7 _____

8 _____

9 _____

10 _____

11 _____

12 _____

13 _____

14 _____

15 _____

Name: _____

(Title) _____

Brainstorm Word List

1 _____

2 _____

3 _____

4 _____

5 _____

6 _____

7 _____

8 _____

9 _____

10 _____

11 _____

12 _____

13 _____

14 _____

15 _____

Historical - Illustration 43

Name: _____

Brainstorm Word List

_____
_____
_____
_____
_____

_____
(Title)

1 _____

2 _____

3 _____

4 _____

5 _____

6 _____

7 _____

8 _____

9 _____

10 _____

11 _____

12 _____

13 _____

14 _____

15 _____

Name: _____

(Title) _____

Brainstorm Word List

1 _____

2 _____

3 _____

4 _____

5 _____

6 _____

7 _____

8 _____

9 _____

10 _____

11 _____

12 _____

13 _____

14 _____

15 _____

Story Starters

Name: _____

Brainstorm Word List

_____
_____
_____
_____
_____

_____
(Title)

1 _____

2 _____

3 _____

4 _____

5 _____

6 _____

7 _____

8 _____

9 _____

10 _____

11 _____

12 _____

13 _____

14 _____

15 _____

Name: _____

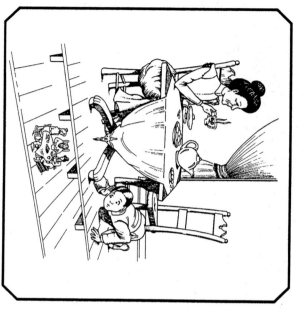

(Title) _____

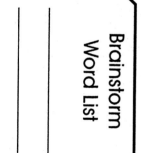

Brainstorm Word List

1. _____
2. _____
3. _____
4. _____
5. _____
6. _____
7. _____
8. _____
9. _____
10. _____
11. _____
12. _____
13. _____
14. _____
15. _____

Fantasy - Illustration 47

Name: _____

Brainstorm
Word List

_____
(Title)

1 _____
2 _____
3 _____
4 _____
5 _____
6 _____
7 _____
8 _____
9 _____
10 _____
11 _____
12 _____
13 _____
14 _____
15 _____

Name: _____

_____
(Title)

Brainstorm Word List

1 _____

2 _____

3 _____

4 _____

5 _____

6 _____

7 _____

8 _____

9 _____

10 _____

11 _____

12 _____

13 _____

14 _____

15 _____

Fantasy - Illustration 49

Name: _____

Brainstorm
Word List

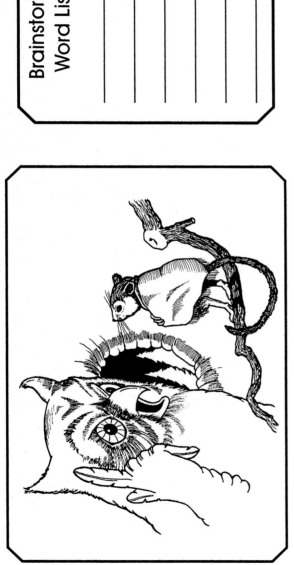

_____ (Title)

1 _____

2 _____

3 _____

4 _____

5 _____

6 _____

7 _____

8 _____

9 _____

10 _____

11 _____

12 _____

13 _____

14 _____

15 _____

Name: _____

Brainstorm Word List

_____
(Title)

1 _____

2 _____

3 _____

4 _____

5 _____

6 _____

7 _____

8 _____

9 _____

10 _____

11 _____

12 _____

13 _____

14 _____

15 _____

Fantasy - Illustration 51

Name: _____

Brainstorm Word List

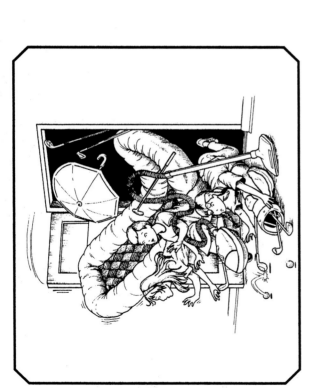

_____
(Title)

1 _____

2 _____

3 _____

4 _____

5 _____

6 _____

7 _____

8 _____

9 _____

10 _____

11 _____

12 _____

13 _____

14 _____

15 _____

Fantasy - Illustration 52

Name: _____

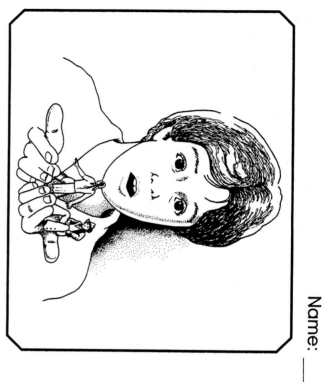

Brainstorm
Word List

_____
(Title)

1. _____
2. _____
3. _____
4. _____
5. _____
6. _____
7. _____
8. _____
9. _____
10. _____
11. _____
12. _____
13. _____
14. _____
15. _____

Story Starters

Name: _____

Brainstorm
Word List

_____
_____
_____
_____
_____
_____

_____
(Title)

1 _____
2 _____
3 _____
4 _____
5 _____
6 _____
7 _____
8 _____
9 _____
10 _____
11 _____
12 _____
13 _____
14 _____
15 _____

Name: _____

_____
(Title)

© On The Mark Press • S&S Learning Materials

60

Fantasy - Illustration 55

Brainstorm Word List

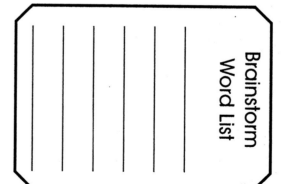

1 _____

2 _____

3 _____

4 _____

5 _____

6 _____

7 _____

8 _____

9 _____

10 _____

11 _____

12 _____

13 _____

14 _____

15 _____

Story Starters

Name: _____

Brainstorm
Word List

_____
_____
_____
_____
_____

_____ (Title)

1 _____
2 _____
3 _____
4 _____
5 _____
6 _____
7 _____
8 _____
9 _____
10 _____
11 _____
12 _____
13 _____
14 _____
15 _____

Name: _____

(Title) _____

Brainstorm Word List

1 _____

2 _____

3 _____

4 _____

5 _____

6 _____

7 _____

8 _____

9 _____

10 _____

11 _____

12 _____

13 _____

14 _____

15 _____

Fantasy - Illustration 57

Name: _____

Brainstorm
Word List

_____
_____
_____
_____
_____
_____

(Title) _____

1 _____
2 _____
3 _____
4 _____
5 _____
6 _____
7 _____
8 _____
9 _____
10 _____
11 _____
12 _____
13 _____
14 _____
15 _____

Fantasy - Illustration 58

Story Starters

Name: _____ Title: _____

1 _____

2 _____

3 _____

4 _____

5 _____

6 _____

7 _____

8 _____

9 _____

10 _____

11 _____

12 _____

13 _____

14 _____

15 _____

16 _____

17 _____

18 _____

19 _____

20 _____

21 _____

22 _____

OTM-1865 • SSR1-65 Story Starters